Percy: A Tragedy by Hannah More

Hannah More was born on February 2nd, 1745 at Fishponds in the parish of Stapleton, near Bristol. She was the fourth of five daughters.

The City of Bristol, at that time, was a centre for slave-trading and Hannah would, over time, become one of its staunchest critics.

She was keen to learn, possessed a sharp intellect and was assiduous in studying. Hannah first wrote in 1762 with The Search after Happiness (by the mid-1780s some 10,000 copies had been sold).

In 1767 Hannah became engaged to William Turner. After six years, with no wedding in sight, the engagement was broken off. Turner then bestowed upon her an annual annuity of £200. This was enough to meet her needs and set her free to pursue a literary career.

Her first play, The Inflexible Captive, was staged at Bath in 1775. The famous David Garrick himself produced her next play, Percy, in 1777 as well as writing both the Prologue and Epilogue for it. It was a great success when performed at Covent Garden in December of that year.

Hannah turned to religious writing with Sacred Dramas in 1782; it rapidly ran through nineteen editions. These and the poems Bas-Bleu and Florio (1786) mark her gradual transition to a more serious and considered view of life.

Hannah contributed much to the newly-founded Abolition Society including, in February 1788, her publication of Slavery, a Poem recognised as one of the most important of the abolition period.

Her work now became more evangelical. In the 1790s she wrote several Cheap Repository Tracts which covered moral, religious and political topics and were both for sale or distributed to literate poor people. The most famous is, perhaps, The Shepherd of Salisbury Plain, describing a family of incredible frugality and contentment. Two million copies of these were circulated, in one year.

In 1789, she purchased a small house at Cowslip Green in Somerset. She was instrumental in setting up twelve schools in the area by 1800.

She continued to oppose slavery throughout her life, but at the time of the Abolition Bill of 1807, her health did not permit her to take as active a role in the movement as she had done in the late 1780s, although she maintained a correspondence with Wilberforce and others.

In July 1833, the Bill to abolish slavery throughout the British Empire passed in the House of Commons, followed by the House of Lords on August 1st.

Hannah More died on September 7th, 1833.

Index of Contents

NOTES

This tragedy, in which Mrs. Hannah More is supposed to have been assisted by Garrick, was produced at Covent Garden Theatre, in 1778, with success; and revived, in 1818, at the same Theatre.
The feuds of the rival houses of Percy and of Douglas have furnished materials for this melancholy tale, in which Mrs. More[1] has embodied many judicious sentiments and excellent passages, producing a forcible lesson to parental tyranny. The victim of her husband's unreasonable jealousy, Elwina's virtuous conflict is pathetic and interesting; while Percy's sufferings, and the vain regret of Earl Raby, excite and increase our sympathy.

[1] Of this estimable lady, a contemporary writer says, "This lady has for many years flourished in the literary world, which she has richly adorned by a variety of labours, all possessing strong marks of excellence. In the cause of religion and society, her labours are original and indefatigable; and the industrious poor have been at once enlightened by her instructions, and supported by her bounty."

As a dramatic writer, Mrs. More is known by her "Search after Happiness," pastoral drama; "The Inflexible Captive,"—"Percy," and "Fatal Falsehood," tragedies; and by her "Sacred Dramas."

DRAMATIS PERSONAE

Percy, Earl of Northumberland	Mr. Lewis.
Earl Douglas	Mr. Wroughton.
Earl Raby, Elwina's Father	Mr. Aickin.
Edric, Friend to Douglas	Mr. Whitefield.
Harcourt, Friend to Percy	Mr. Robson.
Sir Hubert, a Knight	Mr. Hull.
Elwina	Mrs. Barry.
Birtha	Mrs. Jackson.

Knights, Guards, Attendants, &c.

ACT THE FIRST

SCENE I - A GOTHIC HALL

[Enter **EDRIC** and **BIRTHA**.]

BIRTHA
What may this mean? Earl Douglas has enjoin'd thee
To meet him here in private?

EDRIC
Yes, my sister,
And this injunction I have oft receiv'd;
But when he comes, big with some painful secret,
He starts, looks wild, then drops ambiguous hints,
Frowns, hesitates, turns pale, and says 'twas nothing;
Then feigns to smile, and by his anxious care
To prove himself at ease, betrays his pain.

BIRTHA
Since my short sojourn here, I've mark'd this earl,
And though the ties of blood unite us closely,
I shudder at his haughtiness of temper,
Which not his gentle wife, the bright Elwina,
Can charm to rest. Ill are their spirits pair'd;
His is the seat of frenzy, her's of softness,
His love is transport, her's is trembling duty;
Rage in his soul is as the whirlwind fierce,
While her's ne'er felt the power of that rude passion.

EDRIC
Perhaps the mighty soul of Douglas mourns,
Because inglorious love detains him here,
While our bold knights, beneath the Christian standard,
Press to the bulwarks of Jerusalem.

BIRTHA
Though every various charm adorns Elwina,
And though the noble Douglas dotes to madness,
Yet some dark mystery involves their fate:

The canker grief devours Elwina's bloom,
And on her brow meek resignation sits,
Hopeless, yet uncomplaining.

EDRIC
'Tis most strange.

BIRTHA
Once, not long since, she thought herself alone;
'Twas then the pent-up anguish burst its bounds;
With broken voice, clasp'd hands, and streaming eyes,
She call'd upon her father, call'd him cruel,
And said her duty claim'd far other recompence.

EDRIC
Perhaps the absence of the good Lord Raby,
Who, at her nuptials, quitted this fair castle,
Resigning it to her, may thus afflict her.
Hast thou e'er question'd her, good Birtha?

BIRTHA
Often,
But hitherto in vain; and yet she shews me
The endearing kindness of a sister's love;
But if I speak of Douglas—

EDRIC
See! he come
It would offend him should he find you here.

[Enter **DOUGLAS**]

DOUGLAS
How! Edric and his sister in close conference?
Do they not seem alarm'd at my approach?
And see, how suddenly they part! Now Edric,

[Exit **BIRTHA**]

Was this well done? or was it like a friend,
When I desir'd to meet thee here alone;
With all the warmth of trusting confidence,
To lay my bosom naked to thy view,
And shew thee all its weakness, was it well
To call thy sister here, to let her witness
Thy friend's infirmity?—perhaps to tell her—

EDRIC

My lord, I nothing know; I came to learn.

DOUGLAS
Nay then thou dost suspect there's something wrong?

EDRIC
If we were bred from infancy together,
If I partook in all thy youthful griefs,
And every joy thou knew'st was doubly mine,
Then tell me all the secret of thy soul:
Or have these few short months of separation,
The only absence we have ever known,
Have these so rent the bands of love asunder,
That Douglas should distrust his Edric's truth?

DOUGLAS
My friend, I know thee faithful as thou'rt brave,
And I will trust thee—but not now, good Edric,
'Tis past, 'tis gone, it is not worth the telling,
'Twas wrong to cherish what disturb'd my peace;
I'll think of it no more.

EDRIC
Transporting news!
I fear'd some hidden trouble vex'd your quiet.
In secret I have watch'd—

DOUGLAS
Ha! watch'd In secret?
A spy, employ'd, perhaps, to note my actions.
What have I said? Forgive me, thou art noble:
Yet do not press me to disclose my grief,
For when thou know'st it, I perhaps shall hate thee
As much, my Edric, as I hate myself
For my suspicions—I am ill at ease.

EDRIC
How will the fair Elwina grieve to hear it!

DOUGLAS
Hold, Edric, hold—thou hast touch'd the fatal string
That wakes me into madness. Hear me then,
But let the deadly secret be secur'd
With bars of adamant in thy close breast.
Think on the curse which waits on broken oaths;
A knight is bound by more than vulgar ties,
And perjury in thee were doubly damn'd.
Well then, the king of England—

EDRIC
Is expected
From distant Palestine.

DOUGLAS
Forbid it, Heaven!
For with him comes—

EDRIC
Ah! who?

DOUGLAS
Peace, peace,
For see Elwina's here. Retire, my Edric;
When next we meet, thou shalt know all. Farewell.

[Exit **EDRIC**]

Now to conceal with care my bosom's anguish,
And let her beauty chase away my sorrows!
Yes, I would meet her with a face of smiles—
But 'twill not be.

[Enter **ELWINA**]

ELWINA [aside.]
Alas, 'tis ever thus!
Thus ever clouded is his angry brow.

DOUGLAS
I were too blest, Elwina, could I hope
You met me here by choice, or that your bosom
Shar'd the warm transports mine must ever feel
At your approach.

ELWINA
My lord, if I intrude,
The cause which brings me claims at least forgiveness:
I fear you are not well, and come, unbidden,
Except by faithful duty, to inquire,
If haply in my power, my little power,
I have the means to minister relief
To your affliction?

DOUGLAS
What unwonted goodness!
O I were blest above the lot of man,

If tenderness, not duty, brought Elwina;
Cold, ceremonious, and unfeeling duty,
That wretched substitute for love: but know,
The heart demands a heart; nor will be paid
With less than what it gives. E'en now, Elwina,
The glistening tear stands trembling in your eyes,
Which cast their mournful sweetness on the ground,
As if they fear'd to raise their beams to mine,
And read the language of reproachful love.

ELWINA
My lord, I hop'd the thousand daily proofs
Of my obedience—

DOUGLAS
Death to all my hopes!
Heart-rending word!—obedience? what's obedience?
'Tis fear, 'tis hate, 'tis terror, 'tis aversion,
'Tis the cold debt of ostentatious duty,
Paid with insulting caution, to remind me
How much you tremble to offend a tyrant
So terrible as Douglas.—O, Elwina—
While duty measures the regard it owes
With scrupulous precision and nice justice,
Love never reasons, but profusely gives,
Gives, like a thoughtless prodigal, its all,
And trembles then, lest it has done too little.

ELWINA
Indeed I'm most unhappy that my cares,
And my solicitude to please, offend.

DOUGLAS
True tenderness is less solicitous,
Less prudent and more fond; the enamour'd heart,
Conscious it loves, and blest in being lov'd,
Reposes on the object it adores,
And trusts the passion it inspires and feels.—
Thou hast not learnt how terrible it is
To feed a hopeless flame.—But hear, Elwina,
Thou most obdurate, hear me.—

ELWINA
Say, my lord,
For your own lips shall vindicate my fame,
Since at the altar I became your wife,
Can malice charge me with an act, a word,
I ought to blush at? Have I not still liv'd

As open to the eye of observation,
As fearless innocence should ever live?
I call attesting angels to be witness,
If in my open deed, or secret thought,
My conduct, or my heart, they've aught discern'd
Which did not emulate their purity.

DOUGLAS

This vindication ere you were accus'd,
This warm defence, repelling all attacks
Ere they are made, and construing casual words
To formal accusations, trust me, madam,
Shews rather an alarm'd and vigilant spirit,
For ever on the watch to guard its secret,
Than the sweet calm of fearless innocence.
Who talk'd of guilt? Who testified suspicion?

ELWINA

Learn, sir, that virtue, while 'tis free from blame,
Is modest, lowly, meek, and unassuming;
Not apt, like fearful vice, to shield its weakness
Beneath the studied pomp of boastful phrase
Which swells to hide the poverty it shelters;
But, when this virtue feels itself suspected,
Insulted, set at nought, its whiteness stain'd,
It then grows proud, forgets its humble worth,
And rates itself above its real value.

DOUGLAS

I did not mean to chide! but think, O think,
What pangs must rend this fearful doting heart,
To see you sink impatient of the grave,
To feel, distracting thought! to feel you hate me!

ELWINA

What if the slender thread by which I hold
This poor precarious being soon must break,
Is it Elwina's crime, or heaven's decree?
Yet I shall meet, I trust, the king of terrors,
Submissive and resign'd, without one pang,
One fond regret, at leaving this gay world.

DOUGLAS

Yes, madam, there is one, one man ador'd,
For whom your sighs will heave, your tears will flow,
For whom this hated world will still be dear,
For whom you still would live—

ELWINA
Hold, hold, my lord,
What may this mean?

DOUGLAS
Ah! I have gone too far.
What have I said?—Your father, sure, your father,
The good Lord Raby, may at least expect
One tender sigh.

ELWINA
Alas, my lord! I thought
The precious incense of a daughter's sighs
Might rise to heaven, and not offend its ruler.

DOUGLAS
'Tis true; yet Raby is no more belov'd
Since he bestow'd his daughter's hand on Douglas:
That was a crime the dutiful Elwina
Can never pardon; and believe me, madam,
My love's so nice, so delicate my honour,
I am asham'd to owe my happiness
To ties which make you wretched.

[Exit **DOUGLAS**]

ELWINA
Ah! how's this?
Though I have ever found him fierce and rash,
Full of obscure surmises and dark hints,
Till now he never ventur'd to accuse me.
Yet there is one, one man belov'd, ador'd,
For whom your tears will flow—these were his words—
And then the wretched subterfuge of, Raby—
How poor th' evasion!—But my Birtha come.

[Enter **BIRTHA**]

BIRTHA
Crossing the portico I met Lord Douglas,
Disorder'd were his looks, his eyes shot fire;
He call'd upon your name with such distraction,
I fear'd some sudden evil had befallen you.

ELWINA
Not sudden: no; long has the storm been gathering,
Which threatens speedily to burst in ruin
On this devoted head.

BIRTHA

I ne'er beheld
Your gentle soul so ruffled, yet I've mark'd you,
While others thought you happiest of the happy,
Blest with whate'er the world calls great, or good,
With all that nature, all that fortune gives,
I've mark'd you bending with a weight of sorrow.

ELWINA

O I will tell thee all! thou couldst not find
An hour, a moment in Elwina's life,
When her full heart so long'd to ease its burthen,
And pour its sorrows in thy friendly bosom:
Hear then, with pity hear, my tale of woe,
And, O forgive, kind nature, filial piety,
If my presumptuous lips arraign a father!
Yes, Birtha, that belov'd, that cruel father,
Has doom'd me to a life of hopeless anguish,
To die of grief ere half my days are number'd;
Doom'd me to give my trembling hand to Douglas,
'Twas all I had to give—my heart was—Percy's.

BIRTHA

What do I hear?

ELWINA

My misery, not my crime.
Long since the battle 'twixt the rival houses
Of Douglas and of Percy, for whose hate
This mighty globe's too small a theatre,
One summer's morn my father chas'd the deer
On Cheviot Hills, Northumbria's fair domain.

BIRTHA

On that fam'd spot where first the feuds commenc'd
Between the earls?

ELWINA

The same. During the chace,
Some of my father's knights receiv'd an insult
From the Lord Percy's herdsmen, churlish foresters,
Unworthy of the gentle blood they serv'd.
My father, proud and jealous of his honour,
(Thou know'st the fiery temper of our barons,)
Swore that Northumberland had been concern'd
In this rude outrage, nor would hear of peace,
Or reconcilement, which the Percy offer'd;

But bade me hate, renounce, and banish him.
O! 'twas a task too hard for all my duty:
I strove, and wept; I strove—but still I lov'd.

BIRTHA
Indeed 'twas most unjust; but say what follow'd?

ELWINA
Why should I dwell on the disastrous tale?
Forbid to see me, Percy soon embark'd
With our great king against the Saracen.
Soon as the jarring kingdoms were at peace,
Earl Douglas, whom till then I ne'er had seen,
Came to this castle; 'twas my hapless fate
To please him.—Birtha! thou can'st tell what follow'd:
But who shall tell the agonies I felt?
My barbarous father forc'd me to dissolve
The tender vows himself had bid me form—
He dragg'd me trembling, dying, to the altar,
I sigh'd, I struggled, fainted, and complied.

BIRTHA
Did Douglas know, a marriage had been once
Propos'd 'twixt you and Percy?

ELWINA
If he did,
He thought, like you, it was a match of policy,
Nor knew our love surpass'd our fathers' prudence.

BIRTHA
Should he now find he was the instrument
Of the Lord Raby's vengeance?

ELWINA
'Twere most dreadful!
My father lock'd this motive in his breast,
And feign'd to have forgot the chace of Cheviot.
Some moons have now completed their slow course
Since my sad marriage.—Percy still is absent.

BIRTHA
Nor will return before his sov'reign come.

ELWINA
Talk not of his return! this coward heart
Can know no thought of peace but in his absence.
How, Douglas here again? some fresh alarm!

[Enter **DOUGLAS**, agitated, with letters in his hand]

DOUGLAS
Madam, your pardon—

ELWINA
What disturbs my lord?

DOUGLAS
Nothing.—Disturb! I ne'er was more at ease.
These letters from your father give us notice
He will be here to-night:—He further adds,
The king's each hour expected.

ELWINA
How? the king?
Said you, the king?

DOUGLAS
And 'tis Lord Raby's pleasure
That you among the foremost bid him welcome.
You must attend the court.

ELWINA
Must I, my lord?

DOUGLAS [aside.]
Now to observe how she receives the news!

ELWINA
I must not,—cannot.—By the tender love
You have so oft profess'd for poor Elwina,
Indulge this one request—O let me stay!

DOUGLAS [aside.]
Enchanting sounds! she does not wish to go—

ELWINA
The bustling world, the pomp which waits on greatness,
Ill suits my humble, unambitious soul;—
Then leave me here, to tread the safer path
Of private life; here, where my peaceful course
Shall be as silent as the shades around me;
Nor shall one vagrant wish be e'er allow'd
To stray beyond the bounds of Raby Castle.

DOUGLAS

O music to my ears! [aside.] Can you resolve
To hide those wond'rous beauties in the shade,
Which rival kings would cheaply buy with empire?
Can you renounce the pleasures of a court,
Whose roofs resound with minstrelsy and mirth?

ELWINA
My lord, retirement is a wife's best duty,
And virtue's safest station is retreat.

DOUGLAS
My soul's in transports!
[aside]
But can you forego
What wins the soul of woman—admiration?
A world, where charms inferior far to yours
Only presume to shine when you are absent!
Will you not long to meet the public gaze?
Long to eclipse the fair, and charm the brave?

ELWINA
These are delights in which the mind partakes not.

DOUGLAS[aside.]
I'll try her farther.

[Takes her hand, and looks stedfastly at her as he speaks]

But reflect once more:
When you shall hear that England's gallant peers,
Fresh from the fields of war, and gay with glory,
All vain with conquest, and elate with fame,
When you shall hear these princely youths contend,
In many a tournament, for beauty's prize;
When you shall hear of revelry and masking,
Of mimic combats and of festive halls,
Of lances shiver'd in the cause of love,
Will you not then repent, then wish your fate,
Your happier fate, had till that hour reserv'd you
For some plumed conqueror?

ELWINA
My fate, my lord,
Is now bound up with yours.

DOUGLAS
Here let me kneel—
Yes, I will kneel, and gaze, and weep, and wonder;

Thou paragon of goodness!—pardon, pardon,

[Kisses her hand]

I am convinc'd—I can no longer doubt,
Nor talk, nor hear, nor reason, nor reflect.
—I must retire, and give a loose to joy.

[Exit **DOUGLAS**]

BIRTHA
The king returns.

ELWINA
And with him Percy comes!

BIRTHA
You needs must go.

ELWINA
Shall I solicit ruin,
And pull destruction on me ere its time?
I, who have held it criminal to name him?
I will not go—I disobey thee, Douglas,
But disobey thee to preserve thy honour.

[Exeunt]

ACT II

SCENE I - THE HALL

DOUGLAS
See that the traitor instantly be seiz'd,
And strictly watch'd: let none have access to him.—
O jealousy, thou aggregate of woes!
Were there no hell, thy torments would create one.
But yet she may be guiltless—may? she must.
How beautiful she look'd! pernicious beauty!
Yet innocent as bright seem'd the sweet blush
That mantled on her cheek. But not for me,
But not for me, those breathing roses blow!
And then she wept—What! can I bear her tears?
Well—let her weep—her tears are for another;
O did they fall for me, to dry their streams
I'd drain the choicest blood that feeds this heart,

Nor think the drops I shed were half so precious.

[He stands in a musing posture]

[Enter **LORD RABY**]

LORD RABY
Sure I mistake—am I in Raby Castle?
Impossible; that was the seat of smiles;
And Cheerfulness and Joy were household gods.
I us'd to scatter pleasures when I came,
And every servant shar'd his lord's delight;
But now Suspicion and Distrust dwell here,
And Discontent maintains a sullen sway.
Where is the smile unfeign'd, the jovial welcome,
Which cheer'd the sad, beguil'd the pilgrim's pain,
And made Dependency forget its bonds?
Where is the antient, hospitable hall,
Whose vaulted roof once rung with harmless mirth,
Where every passing stranger was a guest,
And every guest a friend? I fear me much,
If once our nobles scorn their rural seats,
Their rural greatness, and their vassals' love,
Freedom and English grandeur are no more.

DOUGLAS [advancing]
My lord, you are welcome.

LORD RABY
Sir, I trust I am;
But yet methinks I shall not feel I'm welcome
Till my Elwina bless me with her smiles:
She was not wont with ling'ring step to meet me,
Or greet my coming with a cold embrace;
Now, I extend my longing arms in vain;
My child, my darling, does not come to fill them.
O they were happy days, when she would fly
To meet me from the camp, or from the chace,
And with her fondness overpay my toils!
How eager would her tender hands unbrace
The ponderous armour from my war-worn limbs,
And pluck the helmet which oppos'd her kiss!

DOUGLAS
O sweet delights, that never must be mine!

LORD RABY
What do I hear?

DOUGLAS
Nothing: inquire no farther.

LORD RABY
My lord, if you respect an old man's peace,
If e'er you doted on my much-lov'd child,
As 'tis most sure you made me think you did,
Then, by the pangs which you may one day feel,
When you, like me, shall be a fond, fond father,
And tremble for the treasure of your age,
Tell me what this alarming silence means?
You sigh, you do not speak, nay more, you hear not;
Your lab'ring soul turns inward on itself,
As there were nothing but your own sad thoughts
Deserv'd regard. Does my child live?

DOUGLAS
She does.

LORD RABY
To bless her father!

DOUGLAS
And to curse her husband!

LORD RABY
Ah! have a care, my lord, I'm not so old—

DOUGLAS
Nor I so base, that I should tamely bear it;
Nor am I so inur'd to infamy,
That I can say, without a burning blush,
She lives to be my curse!

LORD RABY
How's this?

DOUGLAS
I thought
The lily opening to the heaven's soft dews,
Was not so fragrant, and was not so chaste.

LORD RABY
Has she prov'd otherwise? I'll not believe it,
Who has traduc'd my sweet, my innocent child?
Yet she's too good to 'scape calumnious tongues.
I know that Slander loves a lofty mark:

It saw her soar a flight above her fellows,
And hurl'd its arrow to her glorious height,
To reach her heart, and bring her to the ground.

DOUGLAS
Had the rash tongue of Slander so presum'd,
My vengeance had not been of that slow sort
To need a prompter; nor should any arm,
No, not a father's, dare dispute with mine,
The privilege to die in her defence.
None dares accuse Elwina, but—

LORD RABY
But who?

DOUGLAS
But Douglas.

LORD RABY [Puts his hand to his sword]
You?—O spare my age's weakness!
You do not know what 'tis to be a father;
You do not know, or you would pity me,
The thousand tender throbs, the nameless feelings,
The dread to ask, and yet the wish to know,
When we adore and fear; but wherefore fear?
Does not the blood of Raby fill her veins?

DOUGLAS
Percy;—know'st thou that name?

LORD RABY
How? What of Percy?

DOUGLAS
He loves Elwina, and, my curses on him!
He is belov'd again.

LORD RABY
I'm on the rack!

DOUGLAS
Not the two Theban brothers bore each other
Such deep, such deadly hate as I and Percy.

LORD RABY
But tell me of my child.

DOUGLAS [Not minding him]

As I and Percy!
When at the marriage rites, O rites accurs'd!
I seiz'd her trembling hand, she started back,
Cold horror thrill'd her veins, her tears flow'd fast.
Fool that I was, I thought 'twas maiden fear;
Dull, doting ignorance! beneath those terrors,
Hatred for me and love for Percy lurk'd.

LORD RABY
What proof of guilt is this?

DOUGLAS
E'er since our marriage,
Our days have still been cold and joyless all;
Painful restraint, and hatred ill disguis'd,
Her sole return for all my waste of fondness.
This very morn I told her 'twas your will
She should repair to court; with all those graces,
Which first subdued my soul, and still enslave it,
She begg'd to stay behind in Raby Castle,
For courts and cities had no charms for her.
Curse my blind love! I was again ensnar'd,
And doted on the sweetness which deceiv'd me.
Just at the hour she thought I should be absent,
(For chance could ne'er have tim'd their guilt so well,)
Arriv'd young Harcourt, one of Percy's knights,
Strictly enjoin'd to speak to none but her;
I seiz'd the miscreant: hitherto he's silent,
But tortures soon shall force him to confess!

LORD RABY
Percy is absent—They have never met.

DOUGLAS
At what a feeble hold you grasp for succour!
Will it content me that her person's pure?
No, if her alien heart dotes on another,
She is unchaste, were not that other Percy.
Let vulgar spirits basely wait for proof,
She loves another—'tis enough for Douglas.

LORD RABY
Be patient.

DOUGLAS
Be a tame convenient husband,
And meanly wait for circumstantial guilt?
No—I am nice as the first Caesar was,

And start at bare suspicion.

[Going]

LORD RABY [Holding him]
Douglas, hear me;
Thou hast nam'd a Roman husband; if she's false,
I mean to prove myself a Roman father.

[Exit **DOUGLAS**]

This marriage was my work, and thus I'm punish'd!

[Enter **ELWINA**]

ELWINA
Where is my father? let me fly to meet him,
O let me clasp his venerable knees,
And die of joy in his belov'd embrace!

LORD RABY [Avoiding her embrace]
Elwina!

ELWINA
And is that all? so cold?

LORD RABY [Sternly]
Elwina!

ELWINA
Then I'm undone indeed! How stern his looks!
I will not be repuls'd, I am your child,
The child of that dear mother you ador'd;
You shall not throw me off, I will grow here,
And, like the patriarch, wrestle for a blessing.

LORD RABY [Holding her from him]
Before I take thee in these aged arms,
Press thee with transport to this beating heart,
And give a loose to all a parent's fondness,
Answer, and see thou answer me as truly
As if the dread inquiry came from heaven,—
Does no interior sense of guilt confound thee?
Canst thou lay all thy naked soul before me?
Can thy unconscious eye encounter mine?
Canst thou endure the probe, and never shrink?
Can thy firm hand meet mine, and never tremble?
Art thou prepar'd to meet the rigid Judge?

Or to embrace the fond, the melting, father?

ELWINA
Mysterious Heaven! to what am I reserv'd!

LORD RABY
Should some rash man, regardless of thy fame,
And in defiance of thy marriage vows,
Presume to plead a guilty passion for thee,
What would'st thou do?

ELWINA
What honour bids me do.

LORD RABY
Come to my arms!

[They embrace]

ELWINA
My father!

LORD RABY
Yes, Elwina,
Thou art my child—thy mother's perfect image.

ELWINA
Forgive these tears of mingled joy and doubt;
For why that question? who should seek to please
The desolate Elwina?

LORD RABY
But if any
Should so presume, canst thou resolve to hate him,
Whate'er his name, whate'er his pride of blood,
Whate'er his former arrogant pretensions?

ELWINA
Ha!

LORD RABY
Dost thou falter? Have a care, Elwina.

ELWINA
Sir, do not fear me: am I not your daughter?

LORD RABY
Thou hast a higher claim upon thy honour;

Thou art Earl Douglas' wife.

ELWINA [Weeps]
I am, indeed!

LORD RABY
Unhappy Douglas!

ELWINA
Has he then complain'd?
Has he presum'd to sully my white fame?

LORD RABY
He knows that Percy—

ELWINA
Was my destin'd husband;
By your own promise, by a father's promise,
And by a tie more strong, more sacred still,
Mine, by the fast firm bond of mutual love.

LORD RABY
Now, by my fears, thy husband told me truth.

ELWINA
If he has told thee, that thy only child
Was forc'd a helpless victim to the altar,
Torn from his arms who had her virgin heart,
And forc'd to make false vows to one she hated,
Then I confess that he has told the truth.

LORD RABY
Her words are barbed arrows in my heart.
But 'tis too late. [aside]
Thou hast appointed Harcourt
To see thee here by stealth in Douglas' absence?

ELWINA
No, by my life, nor knew I till this moment
That Harcourt was return'd. Was it for this
I taught my heart to struggle with its feelings?
Was it for this I bore my wrongs in silence?
When the fond ties of early love were broken,
Did my weak soul break out in fond complaints?
Did I reproach thee? Did I call thee cruel?
No—I endur'd it all; and wearied Heaven
To bless the father who destroy'd my peace.

[Enter **MESSENGER**]

MESSENGER
My lord, a knight, Sir Hubert as I think,
But newly landed from the holy wars,
Entreats admittance.

LORD RABY
Let the warrior enter.

[Exit **MESSENGER**]

All private interests sink at his approach;
All selfish cares be for a moment banish'd;
I've now no child, no kindred but my country.

ELWINA
Weak heart, be still, for what hast thou to fear?

[Enter **SIR HERBERT**]

LORD RABY
Welcome, thou gallant knight! Sir Hubert, welcome!
Welcome to Raby Castle!—In one word,
Is the king safe? Is Palestine subdu'd?

SIR HUBERT
The king is safe, and Palestine subdu'd.

LORD RABY
Blest be the God of armies! Now, Sir Hubert,
By all the saints, thou'rt a right noble knight!
O why was I too old for this crusade!
I think it would have made me young again,
Could I, like thee, have seen the hated crescent
Yield to the Christian cross.—How now, Elwina!
What! cold at news which might awake the dead?
If there's a drop in thy degenerate veins
That glows not now, thou art not Raby's daughter.
It is religion's cause, the cause of Heaven!

ELWINA
When policy assumes religion's name,
And wears the sanctimonious garb of faith
Only to colour fraud, and license murder,
War then is tenfold guilt.

LORD RABY

Blaspheming girl!

ELWINA
'Tis not the crosier, nor the pontiff's robe,
The saintly look, nor elevated eye,
Nor Palestine destroy'd, nor Jordan's banks
Deluged with blood of slaughter'd infidels;
No, nor the extinction of the eastern world,
Nor all the mad, pernicious, bigot rage
Of your crusades, can bribe that Power who sees
The motive with the act. O blind, to think
That cruel war can please the Prince of Peace!
He, who erects his altar in the heart,
Abhors the sacrifice of human blood,
And all the false devotion of that zeal
Which massacres the world he died to save.

LORD RABY
O impious rage! If thou would'st shun my curse,
No more, I charge thee.—Tell me, good Sir Hubert,
Say, have our arms achiev'd this glorious deed,
(I fear to ask,) without much Christian bloodshed?

ELWINA [aside]
Now, Heaven support me!

SIR HUBERT
My good lord of Raby,
Imperfect is the sum of human glory!
Would I could tell thee that the field was won,
Without the death of such illustrious knights
As make the high-flush'd cheek of victory pale.

ELWINA[aside]
Why should I tremble thus?

LORD RABY
Who have we lost?

SIR HUBERT
The noble Clifford, Walsingham, and Grey,
Sir Harry Hastings, and the valiant Pembroke,
All men of choicest note.

LORD RABY
O that my name
Had been enroll'd in such a list of heroes!
If I was too infirm to serve my country,

I might have prov'd my love by dying for her.

ELWINA
Were there no more?

SIR HUBERT
But few of noble blood.
But the brave youth who gain'd the palm of glory,
The flower of knighthood, and the plume of war,
Who bore his banner foremost in the field,
Yet conquer'd more by mercy than the sword,
Was Percy.

ELWINA[aside]
Then he lives!

LORD RABY
Did he? Did Percy?
O gallant boy, then I'm thy foe no more;
Who conquers for my country is my friend!
His fame shall add new glories to a house,
Where never maid was false, nor knight disloyal.

SIR HUBERT
You do embalm him, lady, with your tears:
They grace the grave of glory where he lies—
He died the death of honour.

ELWINA
Said'st thou—died?

SIR HUBERT
Beneath the towers of Solyma he fell.

ELWINA
Oh!

SIR HUBERT
Look to the lady.

[**ELWINA** faints in her father's arms]

LORD RABY
Gentle knight, retire—
'Tis an infirmity of nature in her,
She ever mourns at any tale of blood;
She will be well anon—mean time, Sir Hubert,
You'll grace our castle with your friendly sojourn.

SIR HUBERT
I must return with speed—health to the lady.

[Exit]

LORD RABY
Look up, Elwina. Should her husband come!
Yet she revives not.

[Enter **DOUGLAS**]

DOUGLAS
Ha—Elwina fainting!
My lord, I fear you have too harshly chid her.
Her gentle nature could not brook your sternness.
She wakes, she stirs, she feels returning life.
My love!

[He takes her hand]

ELWINA
O Percy!

DOUGLAS [starts]
Do my senses fail me?

ELWINA
My Percy, 'tis Elwina calls.

DOUGLAS
Hell, hell!

LORD RABY
Retire awhile, my daughter.

ELWINA
Douglas here,
My father and my husband?—O for pity—

[Exit, casting a look of anguish on both]

DOUGLAS
Now, now confess she well deserves my vengeance!
Before my face to call upon my foe!

LORD RABY
Upon a foe who has no power to hurt thee—

Earl Percy's slain.

DOUGLAS
I live again.—But hold—
Did she not weep? she did, and wept for Percy.
If she laments him, he's my rival still,
And not the grave can bury my resentment.

LORD RABY
The truly brave are still the truly gen'rous;
Now, Douglas, is the time to prove thee both.
If it be true that she did once love Percy,
Thou hast no more to fear, since he is dead.
Release young Harcourt, let him see Elwina,
'Twill serve a double purpose, 'twill at once
Prove Percy's death, and thy unchang'd affection.
Be gentle to my child, and win her heart
By confidence and unreproaching love.

DOUGLAS
By Heaven, thou counsel'st well! it shall be done.
Go set him free, and let him have admittance
To my Elwina's presence.

LORD RABY
Farewell, Douglas.
Shew thou believ'st her faithful, and she'll prove so.

[Exit]

DOUGLAS
Northumberland is dead—that thought is peace!
Her heart may yet be mine, transporting hope!
Percy was gentle, even a foe avows it,
And I'll be milder than a summer's breeze.
Yes, thou most lovely, most ador'd of women,
I'll copy every virtue, every grace,
Of my bless'd rival, happier even in death
To be thus loved, than living to be scorn'd.

[Exit]

ACT III

SCENE I - A GARDEN AT RABY CASTLE, WITH A BOWER

SIR HUBERT
That Percy lives, and is return'd in safety,
More joys my soul than all the mighty conquests
That sun beheld, which rose on Syria's ruin.

PERCY
I've told thee, good Sir Hubert, by what wonder
I was preserv'd, though number'd with the slain.

SIR HUBERT
'Twas strange, indeed!

PERCY
'Twas Heaven's immediate work!
But let me now indulge a dearer joy,
Talk of a richer gift of Mercy's hand;
A gift so precious to my doating heart,
That life preserv'd is but a second blessing.
O Hubert, let my soul indulge its softness!
The hour, the spot, is sacred to Elwina.
This was her fav'rite walk; I well remember,
(For who forgets that loves as I have lov'd?)
'Twas in that very bower she gave this scarf,
Wrought by the hand of love! she bound it on,
And, smiling, cried, Whate'er befal us, Percy,
Be this the sacred pledge of faith between us.
I knelt, and swore, call'd every power to witness,
No time, nor circumstance, should force it from me,
But I would lose my life and that together—
Here I repeat my vow.

SIR HUBERT
Is this the man
Beneath whose single arm an host was crush'd?
He, at whose name the Saracen turn'd pale?
And when he fell, victorious armies wept,
And mourn'd a conquest they had bought so dear?
How has he chang'd the trumpet's martial note,
And all the stirring clangor of the war,
For the soft melting of the lover's lute!
Why are thine eyes still bent upon the bower?

PERCY
O Hubert, Hubert, to a soul enamour'd,
There is a sort of local sympathy,
Which, when we view the scenes of early passion,
Paints the bright image of the object lov'd
In stronger colours than remoter scenes

Could ever paint it; realizes shade,
Dresses it up in all the charms it wore,
Talks to it nearer, frames its answers kinder,
Gives form to fancy, and embodies thought.

SIR HUBERT
I should not be believ'd in Percy's camp,
If I should tell them that their gallant leader,
The thunder of the war, the bold Northumberland,
Renouncing Mars, dissolv'd in amorous wishes,
Loiter'd in shades, and pin'd in rosy bowers,
To catch a transient gleam of two bright eyes.

PERCY
Enough of conquest, and enough of war!
Ambition's cloy'd—the heart resumes its rights.
When England's king, and England's good, requir'd,
This arm not idly the keen falchion brandish'd:
Enough—for vaunting misbecomes a soldier.
I live, I am return'd—am near Elwina!
Seest thou those turrets? Yes, that castle holds her;
But wherefore tell thee this? for thou hast seen her.
How look'd, what said she? Did she hear the tale
Of my imagin'd death without emotion?

SIR HUBERT
Percy, thou hast seen the musk-rose, newly blown,
Disclose its bashful beauties to the sun,
Till an unfriendly, chilling storm descended,
Crush'd all its blushing glories in their prime,
Bow'd its fair head, and blasted all its sweetness;
So droop'd the maid beneath the cruel weight
Of my sad tale.

PERCY
So tender and so true!

SIR HUBERT
I left her fainting in her father's arms,
The dying flower yet hanging on the tree.
Even Raby melted at the news I brought,
And envy'd thee thy glory.

PERCY
Then I am blest!
His hate subdued, I've nothing more to fear.

SIR HUBERT

My embassy dispatch'd, I left the castle,
Nor spoke to any of Lord Raby's household,
For fear the king should chide the tardiness
Of my return. My joy to find you living
You have already heard.

PERCY
But where is Harcourt?
Ere this he should have seen her, told her all,
How I surviv'd, return'd—and how I love!
I tremble at the near approach of bliss,
And scarcely can sustain the joy which waits me.

SIR HUBERT
Grant, Heaven, the fair one prove but half so true!

PERCY
O she is truth itself!

SIR HUBERT
She may be chang'd,
Spite of her tears, her fainting, and alarms.
I know the sex, know them as nature made 'em,
Not such as lovers wish and poets feign.

PERCY
To doubt her virtue were suspecting Heaven,
'Twere little less than infidelity!
And yet I tremble. Why does terror shake
These firm-strung nerves? But 'twill be ever thus,
When fate prepares us more than mortal bliss,
And gives us only human strength to bear it.

SIR HUBERT
What beam of brightness breaks through yonder gloom?

PERCY
Hubert—she comes! by all my hopes, she comes!
'Tis she—the blissful vision is Elwina!
But ah! what mean those tears?—She weeps for me!
O transport!—go.—I'll listen unobserv'd,
And for a moment taste the precious joy,
The banquet of a tear which falls for love.

[Exit **SIR HUBERT. PERCY** goes into the bower]

[Enter **ELWINA**]

Shall I not weep? and have I then no cause?
If I could break the eternal bands of death,
And wrench the sceptre from his iron grasp;
If I could bid the yawning sepulchre
Restore to life its long committed dust;
If I could teach the slaughtering hand of war
To give me back my dear, my murder'd Percy,
Then I indeed might once more cease to weep.

[**PERCY** comes out of the bower]

PERCY
Then cease, for Percy lives.

ELWINA
Protect me, Heaven!

PERCY
O joy unspeakable! My life, my love!
End of my toils, and crown of all my cares!
Kind as consenting peace, as conquest bright,
Dearer than arms, and lovelier than renown!

ELWINA
It is his voice—it is, it is, my Percy!
And dost thou live?

PERCY
I never liv'd till now.

ELWINA
And did my sighs, and did my sorrows, reach thee?
And art thou come at last to dry my tears?
How did'st thou 'scape the fury of the foe?

PERCY
Thy guardian genius hover'd o'er the field,
And turn'd the hostile spear from Percy's breast,
Lest thy fair image should be wounded there.
But Harcourt should have told thee all my fate,
How I surviv'd—

ELWINA
Alas! I have not seen him.
Oh! I have suffer'd much.

PERCY
Of that no more;

For every minute of our future lives
Shall be so bless'd, that we will learn to wonder
How we could ever think we were unhappy.

ELWINA
Percy—I cannot speak.

PERCY
Those tears how eloquent!
I would not change this motionless, mute, joy
For the sweet strains of angels: I look down
With pity on the rest of human kind,
However great may be their fame of happiness,
And think their niggard fate has given them nothing,
Not giving thee; or, granting some small blessing,
Denies them my capacity to feel it.

ELWINA
Alas! what mean you?

PERCY
Can I speak my meaning?
'Tis of such magnitude that words would wrong it;
But surely my Elwina's faithful bosom
Should beat in kind responses of delight,
And feel, but never question, what I mean.

ELWINA
Hold, hold, my heart, thou hast much more to suffer!

PERCY
Let the slow form, and tedious ceremony,
Wait on the splendid victims of ambition.
Love stays for none of these. Thy father's soften'd,
He will forget the fatal Cheviot chace;
Raby is brave, and I have serv'd my country;
I would not boast, it was for thee I conquer'd;
Then come, my love.

ELWINA
O never, never, never!

PERCY
Am I awake? Is that Elwina's voice?

ELWINA
Percy, thou most ador'd, and most deceiv'd!
If ever fortitude sustain'd thy soul,

When vulgar minds have sank beneath the stroke,
Let thy imperial spirit now support thee.—
If thou canst be so wond'rous merciful,
Do not, O do not, curse me!—but thou wilt,
Thou must—for I have done a fearful deed,
A deed of wild despair, a deed of horror.
I am, I am—

PERCY
Speak, say, what art thou?

ELWINA
Married!

PERCY
Oh!

ELWINA
Percy, I think I begg'd thee not to curse me;
But now I do revoke the fond petition.
Speak! ease thy bursting soul; reproach, upbraid,
O'erwhelm me with thy wrongs—I'll bear it all.

PERCY
Open, thou earth, and hide me from her sight!
Did'st thou not bid me curse thee?

ELWINA
Mercy! mercy!

PERCY
And have I 'scap'd the Saracen's fell sword
Only to perish by Elwina's guilt?
I would have bared my bosom to the foe,
I would have died, had I but known you wish'd it.

ELWINA
Percy, I lov'd thee most when most I wrong'd thee;
Yes, by these tears I did.

PERCY
Married! just Heaven!
Married! to whom? Yet wherefore should I know?
It cannot add fresh horrors to thy crime,
Or my destruction.

ELWINA
Oh! 'twill add to both.

How shall I tell? Prepare for something dreadful.
Hast thou not heard of—Douglas?

PERCY
Why 'tis well!
Thou awful Power, why waste thy wrath on me?
Why arm omnipotence to crush a worm?
I could have fallen without this waste of ruin.
Married to Douglas! By my wrongs, I like it;
'Tis perfidy complete, 'tis finish'd falsehood,
'Tis adding fresh perdition to the sin,
And filling up the measure of offence!

ELWINA
Oh! 'twas my father's deed! he made his child
An instrument of vengeance on thy head.
He wept and threaten'd, sooth'd me, and commanded.

PERCY
And you complied, most duteously complied!

ELWINA
I could withstand his fury; but his tears,
Ah, they undid me! Percy, dost thou know
The cruel tyranny of tenderness?
Hast thou e'er felt a father's warm embrace?
Hast thou e'er seen a father's flowing tears,
And known that thou could'st wipe those tears away?
If thou hast felt, and hast resisted these,
Then thou may'st curse my weakness; but if not,
Thou canst not pity, for thou canst not judge.

PERCY
Let me not hear the music of thy voice,
Or I shall love thee still; I shall forget
Thy fatal marriage and my savage wrongs.

ELWINA
Dost thou not hate me, Percy?

PERCY
Hate thee? Yes,
As dying martyrs hate the righteous cause
Of that bless'd power for whom they bleed—I hate thee.

[They look at each other with silent agony]

[Enter **HARCOURT**]

HARCOURT
Forgive, my lord, your faithful knight—

PERCY
Come, Harcourt,
Come, and behold the wretch who once was Percy.

HARCOURT
With grief I've learn'd the whole unhappy tale.
Earl Douglas, whose suspicion never sleeps—

PERCY
What, is the tyrant jealous?

ELWINA
Hear him, Percy.

PERCY
I will command my rage—Go on.

HARCOURT
Earl Douglas
Knew, by my arms and my accoutrements,
That I belong'd to you; he question'd much,
And much he menac'd me, but both alike
In vain; he then arrested and confin'd me.

PERCY
Arrest my knight! The Scot shall answer it.

ELWINA
How came you now releas'd?

HARCOURT
Your noble father
Obtain'd my freedom, having learn'd from Hubert
The news of Percy's death. The good old lord,
Hearing the king's return, has left the castle
To do him homage.
[To **PERCY**]
Sir, you had best retire;
Your safety is endanger'd by your stay.
I fear, should Douglas know—

PERCY
Should Douglas know!
Why what new magic's in the name of Douglas,

That it should strike Northumberland with fear?
Go, seek the haughty Scot, and tell him—no—
Conduct me to his presence.

ELWINA
Percy, hold;
Think not 'tis Douglas—'tis—

PERCY
I know it well—
Thou mean'st to tell me 'tis Elwina's husband;
But that inflames me to superior madness.
This happy husband, this triumphant Douglas,
Shall not insult my misery with his bliss.
I'll blast the golden promise of his joys.
Conduct me to him—nay, I will have way—
Come, let us seek this husband.

ELWINA
Percy, hear me.
When I was robb'd of all my peace of mind,
My cruel fortune left me still one blessing,
One solitary blessing, to console me;
It was my fame.—'Tis a rich jewel, Percy,
And I must keep it spotless, and unsoil'd:
But thou wouldst plunder what e'en Douglas spar'd,
And rob this single gem of all its brightness.

PERCY
Go—thou wast born to rule the fate of Percy.
Thou art my conqueror still.

ELWINA
What noise is that?

[**HARCOURT** goes to the side of the stage]

PERCY
Why art thou thus alarm'd?

ELWINA
Alas! I feel
The cowardice and terrors of the wicked,
Without their sense of guilt.

HARCOURT
My lord, 'tis Douglas.

ELWINA
Fly, Percy, and for ever!

PERCY
Fly from Douglas?

ELWINA
Then stay, barbarian, and at once destroy
My life and fame.

PERCY
That thought is death. I go:
My honour to thy dearer honour yields.

ELWINA
Yet, yet thou art not gone!

PERCY
Farewell, farewell!

[Exit **PERCY**.]

ELWINA
I dare not meet the searching eye of Douglas.
I must conceal my terrors.

[**DOUGLAS** at the side with his sword drawn, **EDRIC** holds him]

DOUGLAS
Give me way.

EDRIC
Thou shalt not enter.

DOUGLAS [Struggling with **EDRIC**]
If there were no hell,
It would defraud my vengeance of its edge,
And she should live.

[Breaks from **EDRIC** and comes forward]

Cursed chance! he is not here.

ELWINA [Going]
I dare not meet his fury.

DOUGLAS
See she flies

With every mark of guilt.—Go, search the bower,
[Aside to **EDRIC**]
He shall not thus escape. Madam, return. [aloud]
Now, honest Douglas, learn of her to feign. [aside]
Alone, Elwina? who just parted hence?
[With affected composure]

ELWINA
My lord, 'twas Harcourt; sure you must have met him.

DOUGLAS
O exquisite dissembler! [aside]
No one else!

ELWINA
My lord!

DOUGLAS
How I enjoy her criminal confusion! [aside.]
You tremble, madam.

ELWINA
Wherefore should I tremble?
By your permission Harcourt was admitted;
'Twas no mysterious, secret introduction.

DOUGLAS
And yet you seem alarm'd.—If Harcourt's presence
Thus agitates each nerve, makes every pulse
Thus wildly throb, and the warm tides of blood
Mount in quick rushing tumults to your cheek;
If friendship can excite such strong emotions,
What tremors had a lover's presence caus'd?

ELWINA
Ungenerous man!

DOUGLAS
I feast upon her terrors. [aside]
The story of his death was well contriv'd;
[To her]
But it affects not me; I have a wife,
Compar'd with whom cold Dian was unchaste.

[Takes her hand]

But mark me well—though it concerns not you—
If there's a sin more deeply black than others,

Distinguish'd from the list of common crimes,
A legion in itself, and doubly dear
To the dark prince of hell, it is—hypocrisy.

[Throws her from him, and exit]

ELWINA
Yes, I will bear his fearful indignation!
Thou melting heart, be firm as adamant;
Ye shatter'd nerves, be strung with manly force,
That I may conquer all my sex's weakness,
Nor let this bleeding bosom lodge one thought,
Cherish one wish, or harbour one desire,
That angels may not hear and Douglas know.

[Exit]

ACT IV

SCENE I - THE HALL

[Enter **DOUGLAS**, his sword drawn and bloody in one hand, in the other a letter. **HARCOURT**, wounded]

DOUGLAS
Traitor, no more! this letter shews thy office;
Twice hast thou robb'd me of my dear revenge.
I took thee for thy leader.—Thy base blood
Would stain the noble temper of my sword;
But as the pander to thy master's lust,
Thou justly fall'st by a wrong'd husband's hand.

HARCOURT
Thy wife is innocent.

DOUGLAS
Take him away.

HARCOURT
Percy, revenge my fall!

[Guards bear **HARCOURT** in]

DOUGLAS
Now for the letter!
He begs once more to see her.—So 'tis plain
They have already met!—but to the rest—

[Reads]
"In vain you wish me to restore the scarf;
Dear pledge of love, while I have life I'll wear it,
'Tis next my heart; no power shall force it thence;
Whene'er you see it in another's hand,
Conclude me dead."—My curses on them both!
How tamely I peruse my shame! but thus,
Thus let me tear the guilty characters
Which register my infamy; and thus,
Thus would I scatter to the winds of heaven
The vile complotters of my foul dishonour.

[Tears the letter in the utmost agitation]

[Enter **EDRIC**]

EDRIC
My lord—

DOUGLAS [in the utmost fury, not seeing **EDRIC**]
The scarf!

EDRIC
Lord Douglas.

DOUGLAS [Still not hearing him]
Yes, the scarf!
Percy, I thank thee for the glorious thought!
I'll cherish it; 'twill sweeten all my pangs,
And add a higher relish to revenge!

EDRIC
My lord!

DOUGLAS
How! Edric here?

EDRIC
What new distress?

DOUGLAS
Dost thou expect I should recount my shame,
Dwell on each circumstance of my disgrace,
And swell my infamy into a tale?
Rage will not let me—But—my wife is false.

EDRIC
Art thou convinc'd?

DOUGLAS
The chronicles of hell
Cannot produce a falser.—But what news
Of her cursed paramour?

EDRIC
He has escap'd.

DOUGLAS
Hast thou examin'd every avenue?
Each spot? the grove? the bower, her favourite haunt?

EDRIC
I've search'd them all.

DOUGLAS
He shall be yet pursued.
Set guards at every gate.—Let none depart
Or gain admittance here, without my knowledge.

EDRIC
What can their purpose be?

DOUGLAS
Is it not clear?
Harcourt has raised his arm against my life;
He fail'd; the blow is now reserv'd for Percy;
Then, with his sword fresh reeking from my heart,
He'll revel with that wanton o'er my tomb;
Nor will he bring her aught she'll hold so dear,
As the curs'd hand with which he slew her husband.
But he shall die! I'll drown my rage in blood,
Which I will offer as a rich libation
On thy infernal altar, black revenge!

[Exeunt]

SCENE II - THE GARDEN

[Enter **ELWINA**]

ELWINA
Each avenue is so beset with guards,
And lynx-ey'd Jealousy so broad awake,
He cannot pass unseen. Protect him, heaven!

[Enter **BIRTHA**]

My Birtha, is he safe? has he escap'd?

BIRTHA
I know not. I dispatch'd young Harcourt to him,
To bid him quit the castle, as you order'd,
Restore the scarf, and never see you more.
But how the hard injunction was receiv'd,
Or what has happen'd since, I'm yet to learn.

ELWINA
O when shall I be eas'd of all my cares,
And in the quiet bosom of the grave
Lay down this weary head!—I'm sick at heart!
Should Douglas intercept his flight!

BIRTHA
Be calm;
Douglas this very moment left the castle,
With seeming peace.

ELWINA
Ah, then, indeed there's danger!
Birtha, whene'er Suspicion feigns to sleep,
'Tis but to make its careless prey secure.

BIRTHA
Should Percy once again entreat to see thee,
'Twere best admit him; from thy lips alone
He will submit to hear his final doom
Of everlasting exile.

ELWINA
Birtha, no;
If honour would allow the wife of Douglas
To meet his rival, yet I durst not do it.
Percy! too much this rebel heart is thine:
Too deeply should I feel each pang I gave;
I cannot hate—but I will banish—thee.
Inexorable duly, O forgive,
If I can do no more!

BIRTHA
If he remains,
As I suspect, within the castle walls,
'Twere best I sought him out.

ELWINA

Then tell him, Birtha,
But, Oh! with gentleness, with mercy, tell him,
That we must never, never, meet again.
The purport of my tale must be severe,
But let thy tenderness embalm the wound
My virtue gives. O soften his despair;
But say—we meet no more.

[Enter **PERCY**]

Rash man, he's here!

[She attempts to go, he seizes her hand]

PERCY

I will be heard; nay, fly not; I will speak;
Lost as I am, I will not be denied
The mournful consolation to complain.

ELWINA

Percy, I charge thee, leave me.

PERCY

Tyrant, no:
I blush at my obedience, blush to think
I left thee here alone, to brave the danger
I now return to share.

ELWINA

That danger's past:
Douglas was soon appeas'd; he nothing knows.
Then leave me, I conjure thee, nor again
Endanger my repose. Yet, ere thou goest,
Restore the scarf.

PERCY

Unkind Elwina, never!
'Tis all that's left me of my buried joys,
All which reminds me that I once was happy.
My letter told thee I would ne'er restore it.

ELWINA

Letter! what letter?

PERCY

That I sent by Harcourt.

ELWINA
Which I have ne'er receiv'd. Douglas perhaps—
Who knows?

BIRTHA
Harcourt, t' elude his watchfulness,
Might prudently retire.

ELWINA
Grant heaven it prove so!

[**ELWINA** going, **PERCY** holds her]

PERCY
Hear me, Elwina; the most savage honour
Forbids not that poor grace.

ELWINA
It bids me fly thee.

PERCY
Then, ere thou goest, if we indeed must part,
To sooth the horrors of eternal exile,
Say but—thou pity'st me!

ELWINA [Weeps]
O Percy—pity thee!
Imperious honour;—surely I may pity him.
Yet, wherefore pity? no, I envy thee:
For thou hast still the liberty to weep,
In thee 'twill be no crime: thy tears are guiltless,
For they infringe no duty, stain no honour,
And blot no vow; but mine are criminal,
Are drops of shame which wash the cheek of guilt,
And every tear I shed dishonours Douglas.

PERCY
I swear my jealous love e'en grudges thee
Thy sad pre-eminence in wretchedness.

ELWINA
Rouse, rouse, my slumb'ring virtue! Percy, hear me.
Heaven, when it gives such high-wrought souls as thine,
Still gives as great occasions to exert them.
If thou wast form'd so noble, great, and gen'rous,
'Twas to surmount the passions which enslave
The gross of human-kind.—Then think, O think,

She, whom thou once didst love, is now another's.

PERCY
Go on—and tell me that that other's Douglas.

ELWINA
Whate'er his name, he claims respect from me:
His honour's in my keeping, and I hold
The trust so pure, its sanctity is hurt
E'en by thy presence.

PERCY
Thou again hast conquer'd.
Celestial virtue, like the angel spirit,
Whose flaming sword defended Paradise,
Stands guard on every charm,—Elwina, yes,
To triumph over Douglas, we'll be virtuous.

ELWINA
'Tis not enough to be,—we must appear so:
Great souls disdain the shadow of offence,
Nor must their whiteness wear the stain of guilt.

PERCY
I shall retract—I dare not gaze upon thee;
My feeble virtue staggers, and again
The fiends of jealousy torment and haunt me.
They tear my heart-strings.—Oh!

ELWINA
No more;
But spare my injur'd honour the affront
To vindicate itself.

PERCY
But, love!

ELWINA
But, glory!

PERCY
Enough! a ray of thy sublimer spirit
Has warm'd my dying honour to a flame!
One effort and 'tis done. The world shall say,
When they shall speak of my disastrous love,
Percy deserv'd Elwina though he lost her.
Fond tears, blind me not yet! a little longer,
Let my sad eyes a little longer gaze,

And leave their last beams here.

ELWINA [Turns from him]
I do not weep.

PERCY
Not weep? then why those eyes avoiding mine?
And why that broken voice? those trembling accents?
That sigh which rends my soul?

ELWINA
No more, no more.

PERCY
That pang decides it. Come—I'll die at once;
Thou Power supreme! take all the length of days,
And all the blessings kept in store for me,
And add to her account.—Yet turn once more,
One little look, one last, short glimpse of day,
And then a long dark night.—Hold, hold, my heart,
O break not yet, while I behold her sweetness;
For after this dear, mournful, tender moment,
I shall have nothing more to do with life.

ELWINA
I do conjure thee, go.

PERCY
'Tis terrible to nature!
With pangs like these the soul and body part!
And thus, but oh, with far less agony,
The poor departing wretch still grasps at being,
Thus clings to life, thus dreads the dark unknown,
Thus struggles to the last to keep his hold;
And when the dire convulsive groan of death
Dislodges the sad spirit—thus it stays,
And fondly hovers o'er the form it lov'd.
Once and no more—farewell, farewell!

ELWINA
For ever!

[They look at each other for some time, then exit **PERCY**]

[After a pause]

'Tis past—the conflict's past! retire, my Birtha,
I would address me to the throne of grace.

BIRTHA
May Heaven restore that peace thy bosom wants!

[Exit **BIRTHA**]

ELWINA [Kneels]
Look down, thou, awful, heart-inspecting Judge,
Look down with mercy on thy erring creature,
And teach my soul the lowliness it needs!
And if some sad remains of human weakness
Should sometimes mingle with my best resolves,
O breathe thy spirit on this wayward heart,
And teach me to repent th' intruding sin
In it's first birth of thought!

[Noise within]

What noise is that?
The clash of swords! should Douglas be return'd!

[Enter **DOUGLAS** and **PERCY**, fighting]

DOUGLAS
Yield, villain, yield!

PERCY
Not till this good right arm
Shall fail its master.

DOUGLAS
This to thy heart, then.

PERCY
Defend thy own.

[They fight; **PERCY** disarms **DOUGLAS**]

DOUGLAS
Confusion, death, and hell!

EDRIC [Without]
This way I heard the noise.

[Enter **EDRIC**, and many **KNIGHTS** and **GUARDS**, from every part of the stage]

PERCY
Cursed treachery!

But dearly will I sell my life.

DOUGLAS
Seize on him.

PERCY
I'm taken in the toils.

[**PERCY** is surrounded by **GUARDS**, who take his sword]

DOUGLAS
In the cursed snare
Thou laid'st for me, traitor, thyself art caught.

ELWINA
He never sought thy life.

DOUGLAS
Adulteress, peace!
The villain Harcourt too—but he's at rest.

PERCY
Douglas, I'm in thy power; but do not triumph,
Percy's betray'd, not conquer'd. Come, dispatch me.

ELWINA [To **DOUGLAS**]
O do not, do not, kill him!

PERCY
Madam, forbear;
For by the glorious shades of my great fathers,
Their godlike spirit is not so extinct,
That I should owe my life to that vile Scot.
Though dangers close me round on every side,
And death besets me, I am Percy still.

DOUGLAS
Sorceress, I'll disappoint thee—he shall die,
Thy minion shall expire before thy face,
That I may feast my hatred with your pangs,
And make his dying groans, and thy fond tears,
A banquet for my vengeance.

ELWINA
Savage tyrant!
I would have fallen a silent sacrifice,
So thou had'st spar'd my fame.—I never wrong'd thee.

PERCY

She knew not of my coming;—I alone
Have been to blame—Spite of her interdiction,
I hither came. She's pure as spotless saints.

ELWINA

I will not be excus'd by Percy's crime;
So white my innocence, it does not ask
The shade of others' faults to set it off;
Nor shall he need to sully his fair fame
To throw a brighter lustre round my virtue.

DOUGLAS

Yet he can only die—but death for honour!
Ye powers of hell, who take malignant joy
In human bloodshed, give me some dire means,
Wild as my hate, and desperate as my wrongs!

PERCY

Enough of words. Thou know'st I hate thee, Douglas;
'Tis stedfast, fix'd, hereditary hate,
As thine for me; our fathers did bequeath it
As part of our unalienable birthright,
Which nought but death can end.—Come, end it here.

ELWINA [Kneels]

Hold, Douglas, hold!—not for myself I kneel,
I do not plead for Percy, but for thee:
Arm not thy hand against thy future peace,
Spare thy brave breast the tortures of remorse,—
Stain not a life of unpolluted honour,
For, oh! as surely as thou strik'st at Percy,
Thou wilt for ever stab the fame of Douglas.

PERCY

Finish the bloody work.

DOUGLAS

Then take thy wish.

PERCY

Why dost thou start?

[**PERCY** bares his bosom. **DOUGLAS** advances to stab him, and discovers the scarf]

DOUGLAS

Her scarf upon his breast!
The blasting sight converts me into stone;

Withers my powers like cowardice or age,
Curdles the blood within my shiv'ring veins,
And palsies my bold arm.

PERCY [Ironically to the **KNIGHTS**]
Hear you, his friends!
Bear witness to the glorious, great exploit,
Record it in the annals of his race,
That Douglas, the renown'd—the valiant Douglas,
Fenc'd round with guards, and safe in his own castle,
Surpris'd a knight unarm'd, and bravely slew him.

DOUGLAS [Throwing away his dagger]
'Tis true—I am the very stain of knighthood.
How is my glory dimm'd!

ELWINA
It blazes brighter!
Douglas was only brave—he now is generous!

PERCY
This action has restor'd thee to thy rank,
And makes thee worthy to contend with Percy.

DOUGLAS
Thy joy will be as short as 'tis insulting.
[To **ELWINA**]
And thou, imperious boy, restrain thy boasting.
Thou hast sav'd my honour, not remov'd my hate,
For my soul loaths thee for the obligation.
Give him his sword.

PERCY
Now thou'rt a noble foe,
And in the field of honour I will meet thee,
As knight encount'ring knight.

ELWINA
Stay, Percy, stay,
Strike at the wretched cause of all, strike here,
Here sheath thy thirsty sword, but spare my husband.

DOUGLAS
Turn, madam, and address those vows to me,
To spare the precious life of him you love.
Even now you triumph in the death of Douglas;
Now your loose fancy kindles at the thought,
And, wildly rioting in lawless hope,

Indulges the adultery of the mind.
But I'll defeat that wish.—Guards, bear her in.
Nay, do not struggle.

[She is borne in]

PERCY
Let our deaths suffice,
And reverence virtue in that form inshrin'd.

DOUGLAS
Provoke my rage no farther.—I have kindled
The burning torch of never-dying vengeance
At love's expiring lamp.—But mark me, friends,
If Percy's happier genius should prevail,
And I should fall, give him safe conduct hence,
Be all observance paid him.—Go, I follow thee.
[aside to **EDRIC**]
Within I've something for thy private ear.

PERCY
Now shall this mutual fury be appeas'd!
These eager hands shall soon be drench'd in slaughter!
Yes—like two famish'd vultures snuffing blood,
And panting to destroy, we'll rush to combat;
Yet I've the deepest, deadliest, cause of hate,
I am but Percy, thou'rt—Elwina's husband.

[Exeunt]

ACT V

SCENE I - ELWINA'S APARTMENT

ELWINA
Thou who in judgment still remember'st mercy,
Look down upon my woes, preserve my husband!
Preserve my husband! Ah, I dare not ask it;
My very prayers may pull down ruin on me!
If Douglas should survive, what then becomes
Of—him—I dare not name? And if he conquers,
I've slain my husband. Agonizing state!
When I can neither hope, nor think, nor pray,
But guilt involves me. Sure to know the worst
Cannot exceed the torture of suspense,
When each event is big with equal horror.

[Looks out]

What, no one yet? This solitude is dreadful!
My horrors multiply!

[Enter **BIRTHA**]

Thou messenger of woe!

BIRTHA
Of woe, indeed!

ELWINA
How, is my husband dead?
Oh, speak!

BIRTHA
Your husband lives.

ELWINA
Then farewell, Percy!
He was the tenderest, truest!—Bless him, heaven,
With crowns of glory and immortal joys!

BIRTHA
Still are you wrong; the combat is not over.
Stay, flowing tears, and give me leave to speak.

ELWINA
Thou sayest that Percy and my husband live;
Then why this sorrow?

BIRTHA
What a task is mine!

ELWINA
Thou talk'st as if I were a child in grief,
And scarce acquainted with calamity.
Speak out, unfold thy tale, whate'er it be,
For I am so familiar with affliction,
It cannot come in any shape will shock me.

BIRTHA
How shall I speak? Thy husband—

ELWINA
What of Douglas?

BIRTHA
When all was ready for the fatal combat,
He call'd his chosen knights, then drew his sword,
And on it made them swear a solemn oath,
Confirm'd by every rite religion bids,
That they would see perform'd his last request,
Be it whate'er it would. Alas! they swore.

ELWINA
What did the dreadful preparation mean?

BIRTHA
Then to their hands he gave a poison'd cup,
Compounded of the deadliest herbs and drugs;
Take this, said he, it is a husband's legacy;
Percy may conquer—and—I have a wife!
If Douglas falls, Elwina must not live.

ELWINA
Spirit of Herod! Why, 'twas greatly thought!
'Twas worthy of the bosom which conceiv'd it!
Yet 'twas too merciful to be his own.
Yes, Douglas, yes, my husband, I'll obey thee,
And bless thy genius which has found the means
To reconcile thy vengeance with my peace,
The deadly means to make obedience pleasant.

BIRTHA
O spare, for pity spare, my bleeding heart:
Inhuman to the last! Unnatural poison!

ELWINA
My gentle friend, what is there in a name?
The means are little where the end is kind.
If it disturb thee, do not call it poison;
Call it the sweet oblivion of my cares,
My balm of woe, my cordial of affliction,
The drop of mercy to my fainting soul,
My kind dismission from a world of sorrow,
My cap of bliss, my passport to the skies.

BIRTHA
Hark! what alarm is that?

ELWINA
The combat's over!

[**BIRTHA** goes out]

[**ELWINA** stands in a fixed attitude, her hands clasped.

Now, gracious heaven, sustain me in the trial,
And bow my spirit to thy great decrees!

[Re-enter **BIRTHA**]

[**ELWINA** looks steadfastly at her without speaking.]

BIRTHA
Douglas is fallen.

ELWINA
Bring me the poison.

BIRTHA
Never.

ELWINA
Where are the knights? I summon you—approach!
Draw near, ye awful ministers of fate,
Dire instruments of posthumous revenge!
Come—I am ready; but your tardy justice
Defrauds the injur'd dead.—Go, haste, my friend,
See that the castle be securely guarded,
Let every gate be barr'd—prevent his entrance.

BIRTHA
Whose entrance?

ELWINA
His—the murderer of my husband.

BIRTHA
He's single, we have hosts of friends.

ELWINA
No matter;
Who knows what love and madness may attempt?
But here I swear by all that binds the good,
Never to see him more.—Unhappy Douglas!
O if thy troubled spirit still is conscious
Of our past woes, look down, and hear me swear,
That when the legacy thy rage bequeath'd me
Works at my heart, and conquers struggling nature,
Ev'n in that agony I'll still be faithful.

She who could never love, shall yet obey, thee,
Weep thy hard fate, and die to prove her truth.

BIRTHA
O unexampled virtue!

[A noise without]

ELWINA
Heard you nothing?
By all my fears the insulting conqueror comes.
O save me, shield me!

[Enter **DOUGLAS**]

Heaven and earth, my husband!

DOUGLAS
Yes—
To blast thee with the sight of him thou hat'st,
Of him thou hast wrong'd, adultress, 'tis thy husband.

ELWINA [Kneels]
Blest be the fountain of eternal mercy,
This load of guilt is spar'd me! Douglas lives!
Perhaps both live!
[to **BIRTHA**]
Could I be sure of that,
The poison were superfluous, joy would kill me.

DOUGLAS
Be honest now, for once, and curse thy stars;
Curse thy detested fate which brings thee back
A hated husband, when thy guilty soul
Revell'd in fond, imaginary joys
With my too happy rival; when thou flew'st,
To gratify impatient, boundless passion,
And join adulterous lust to bloody murder;
Then to reverse the scene! polluted woman!
Mine is the transport now, and thine the pang.

ELWINA
Whence sprung the false report that thou had'st fall'n?

DOUGLAS
To give thy guilty breast a deeper wound,
To add a deadlier sting to disappointment,
I rais'd it—I contriv'd—I sent it thee.

ELWINA

Thou seest me bold, but bold in conscious virtue.
—That my sad soul may not be stain'd with blood,
That I may spend my few short hours in peace,
And die in holy hope of Heaven's forgiveness,
Relieve the terrors of my lab'ring breast,
Say I am clear of murder—say he lives,
Say but that little word, that Percy lives,
And Alps and oceans shall divide us ever,
As far as universal space can part us.

DOUGLAS

Canst thou renounce him?

ELWINA

Tell me that he lives,
And thou shall be the ruler of my fate,
For ever hide me in a convent's gloom,
From cheerful day-light, and the haunts of men,
Where sad austerity and ceaseless prayer
Shall share my uncomplaining day between them.

DOUGLAS

O, hypocrite! now, Vengeance, to thy office.
I had forgot—Percy commends him to thee,
And by my hand—

ELWINA

How—by thy hand?

DOUGLAS

Has sent thee
This precious pledge of love.

[He gives her **PERCY'S** scarf]

ELWINA

Then Percy's dead!

DOUGLAS

He is.—O great revenge, thou now art mine!
See how convulsive sorrow rends her frame!
This, this is transport!—injur'd honour now
Receives its vast, its ample retribution.
She sheds no tears, her grief's too highly wrought;
'Tis speechless agony.—She must not faint—
She shall not 'scape her portion of the pain.

No! she shall feel the fulness of distress,
And wake to keen perception of her loss.

BIRTHA
Monster! Barbarian! leave her to her sorrows.

ELWINA [In a low broken voice]
Douglas—think not I faint, because thou see'st
The pale and bloodless cheek of wan despair.
Fail me not yet, my spirits; thou cold heart,
Cherish thy freezing current one short moment,
And bear thy mighty load a little longer.

DOUGLAS
Percy, I must avow it, bravely fought,—
Died as a hero should;—but, as he fell,
(Hear it, fond wanton!) call'd upon thy name,
And his last guilty breath sigh'd out—Elwina!
Come—give a loose to rage, and feed thy soul
With wild complaints, and womanish upbraidings.

ELWINA [In a low solemn voice]
No.
The sorrow's weak that wastes itself in words,
Mine is substantial anguish—deep, not loud;
I do not rave.—Resentment's the return
Of common souls for common injuries.
Light grief is proud of state, and courts compassion;
But there's a dignity in cureless sorrow,
A sullen grandeur which disdains complaint;
Rage is for little wrongs—Despair is dumb.

[Exeunt **ELWINA** and **BIRTHA**]

DOUGLAS
Why this is well! her sense of woe is strong!
The sharp, keen tooth of gnawing grief devours her,
Feeds on her heart, and pays me back my pangs.
Since I must perish 'twill be glorious ruin:
I fall not singly, but, like some proud tower,
I'll crush surrounding objects in the wreck,
And make the devastation wide and dreadful.

[Enter **LORD RABY**]

LORD RABY
O whither shall a wretched father turn?
Where fly for comfort? Douglas, art thou here?

I do not ask for comfort at thy hands.
I'd but one little casket where I lodged
My precious hoard of wealth, and, like an idiot,
I gave my treasure to another's keeping,
Who threw away the gem, nor knew its value,
But left the plunder'd owner quite a beggar.

DOUGLAS
What art thou come to see thy race dishonour'd?
And thy bright sun of glory set in blood?
I would have spar'd thy virtues, and thy age,
The knowledge of her infamy.

LORD RABY
'Tis false.
Had she been base, this sword had drank her blood.

DOUGLAS
Ha! dost thou vindicate the wanton?

LORD RABY
Wanton?
Thou hast defam'd a noble lady's honour—
My spotless child—in me behold her champion:
The strength of Hercules will nerve this arm,
When lifted in defence of innocence.
The daughter's virtue for the father's shield,
Will make old Raby still invincible.

[Offers to draw]

DOUGLAS
Forbear.

LORD RABY
Thou dost disdain my feeble arm,
And scorn my age.

DOUGLAS
There will be blood enough;
Nor need thy wither'd veins, old lord, be drain'd,
To swell the copious stream.

LORD RABY
Thou wilt not kill her?

DOUGLAS
Oh, 'tis a day of horror!

[Enter **EDRIC** and **BIRTHA**]

EDRIC
Where is Douglas?
I come to save him from the deadliest crime
Revenge did ever meditate.

DOUGLAS
What meanest thou?

EDRIC
This instant fly, and save thy guiltless wife.

DOUGLAS
Save that perfidious—

EDRIC
That much-injur'd woman.

BIRTHA
Unfortunate indeed, but O most innocent!

EDRIC
In the last solemn article of death,
That truth-compelling state, when even bad men
Fear to speak falsely, Percy clear'd her fame.

DOUGLAS
I heard him—'Twas the guilty fraud of love.
The scarf, the scarf! that proof of mutual passion,
Given but this day to ratify their crimes!

BIRTHA
What means my lord? This day? That fatal scarf
Was given long since, a toy of childish friendship;
Long ere your marriage, ere you knew Elwina.

LORD RABY
'Tis I am guilty.

DOUGLAS
Ha!

LORD RABY
I,—I alone.
Confusion, honour, pride, parental fondness,
Distract my soul,—Percy was not to blame,

He was—the destin'd husband of Elwina!
He loved her—was belov'd—and I approv'd.
The tale is long.—I chang'd my purpose since,
Forbad their marriage—

DOUGLAS

And confirm'd my mis'ry!
Twice did they meet to-day—my wife and Percy.

LORD RABY

I know it.

DOUGLAS

Ha! thou knew'st of my dishonour?
Thou wast a witness, an approving witness,
At least a tame one!

LORD RABY

Percy came, 'tis true,
A constant, tender, but a guiltless lover!

DOUGLAS

I shall grow mad indeed; a guiltless lover!
Percy, the guiltless lover of my wife!

LORD RABY

He knew not she was married.

DOUGLAS

How? is't possible?

LORD RABY

Douglas, 'tis true; both, both were innocent;
He of her marriage, she of his return.

BIRTHA

But now, when we believ'd thee dead, she vow'd
Never to see thy rival. Instantly,
Not in a state of momentary passion,
But with a martyr's dignity and calmness,
She bade me bring the poison.

DOUGLAS

Had'st thou done it,
Despair had been my portion! Fly, good Birtha,
Find out the suffering saint—describe my penitence,
And paint my vast extravagance of fondness,
Tell her I love as never mortal lov'd—

Tell her I know her virtues, and adore them—
Tell her I come, but dare not seek her presence,
Till she pronounce my pardon.

BIRTHA
I obey.

[Exit **BIRTHA**]

LORD RABY
My child is innocent! ye choirs of saints,
Catch the blest sounds—my child is innocent!

DOUGLAS
O I will kneel, and sue for her forgiveness,
And thou shalt help me plead the cause of love,
And thou shalt weep—she cannot sure refuse
A kneeling husband and a weeping father.
Thy venerable cheek is wet already.

LORD RABY
Douglas! it is the dew of grateful joy!
My child is innocent! I now would die,
Lest fortune should grow weary of her kindness,
And grudge me this short transport.

DOUGLAS
Where, where, is she?
My fond impatience brooks not her delay;
Quick, let me find her, hush her anxious soul,
And sooth her troubled spirit into peace.

[Enter **BIRTHA**]

BIRTHA
O horror, horror, horror!

DOUGLAS
Ah! what mean'st thou?

BIRTHA
Elwina—

DOUGLAS
Speak—

BIRTHA
Her grief wrought up to frenzy,

She has, in her delirium, swallow'd poison!

LORD RABY
Frenzy and poison!

DOUGLAS
Both a husband's gift;
But thus I do her justice.

[As **DOUGLAS** goes to stab himself, enter **ELWINA** distracted, her hair dishevelled, **PERCY'S** scarf in her hand]

ELWINA [Goes up to **DOUGLAS**]
What, blood again? We cannot kill him twice!
Soft, soft—no violence—he's dead already;—
I did it—Yes—I drown'd him with my tears;
But hide the cruel deed! I'll scratch him out
A shallow grave, and lay the green sod on it;
Ay—and I'll bind the wild briar o'er the turf,
And plant a willow there, a weeping willow—

[She sits on the ground]

But look you tell not Douglas, he'll disturb him;
He'll pluck the willow up—and plant a thorn.
He will not let me sit upon his grave,
And sing all day, and weep and pray all night.

LORD RABY
Dost thou not know me?

ELWINA
Yes—I do remember
You had a harmless lamb.

LORD RABY
I had indeed!

ELWINA
From all the flock you chose her out a mate,
In sooth a fair one—you did bid her love it—
But while the shepherd slept, the wolf devour'd it.

LORD RABY
My heart will break. This is too much, too much!

ELWINA [Smiling]
O 'twas a cordial draught—I drank it all.

LORD RABY
What means my child?

DOUGLAS
The poison! Oh the poison!
Thou dear wrong'd innocence—

ELWINA
Off—murderer, off!
Do not defile me with those crimson hands.

[Shews the scarf]

This is his winding sheet—I'll wrap him in it—
I wrought it for my love—there—now I've drest him.
How brave he looks! my father will forgive him,
He dearly lov'd him once—but that is over.
See where he comes—beware, my gallant Percy,
Ah! come not here, this is the cave of death,
And there's the dark, dark palace of Revenge!
See the pale king sits on his blood-stain'd throne!
He points to me—I come, I come, I come.

[She faints, they run to her, **DOUGLAS** takes up his sword and stabs himself]

DOUGLAS
Thus, thus I follow thee.

EDRIC
Hold thy rash hand!

DOUGLAS
It is too late. No remedy but this
Could medicine a disease so desperate.

LORD RABY
Ah, she revives!

DOUGLAS [Raising himself]
She lives! bear, bear me to her!
We shall be happy yet.

[He struggles to get to her, but sinks down]

It will not be—
O for a last embrace—Alas! I faint—
She lives—Now death is terrible indeed—

Fair spirit, I lov'd thee—O—Elwina!

[Dies]

ELWINA
Where have I been? The damps of death are on me.

LORD RABY
Look up, my child! O do not leave me thus!
Pity the anguish of thy aged father.
Hast thou forgot me?

ELWINA
No—you are my father;
O you are kindly come to close my eyes,
And take the kiss of death from my cold lips!

LORD RABY
Do we meet thus?

ELWINA
We soon shall meet in peace.
I've but a faint remembrance of the past—
But something tells me—O those painful struggles!
Raise me a little—there—

[She sees the body of **DOUGLAS**]

What sight is that?
A sword, and bloody? Ah! and Douglas murder'd!

EDRIC
Convinc'd too late of your unequall'd virtues,
And wrung with deep compunction for your wrongs,
By his own hand the wretched Douglas fell.

ELWINA
This adds another, sharper pang to death.
O thou Eternal! take him to thy mercy,
Nor let this sin be on his head, or mine!

LORD RABY
I have undone you all—the crime is mine!
O thou poor injur'd saint, forgive thy father,
He kneels to his wrong'd child.

ELWINA
Now you are cruel.

Come near, my father, nearer—I would see you,
But mists and darkness cloud my failing sight.
O Death! suspend thy rights for one short moment,
Till I have ta'en a father's last embrace—
A father's blessing.—Once—and now 'tis over.
Receive me to thy mercy, gracious Heaven!

[She dies]

LORD RABY
She's gone! for ever gone! cold, dead and cold.
Am I a father? Fathers love their children—
I murder mine! With impious pride I snatch'd
The bolt of vengeance from the hand of Heaven.
My punishment is great—but oh! 'tis just.
My soul submissive bows. A righteous God
Has made my crime become my chastisement.

[Exeunt]

Hannah More - A Short Biography

Hannah More was born on February 2nd, 1745 at Fishponds in the parish of Stapleton, near Bristol. She was the fourth of five daughters of Jacob More, a schoolmaster. He was originally from a family of Presbyterians in Norfolk, but had become a member of the Church of England to pursue a career in the Church. After losing a lawsuit over an estate he had hoped to inherit, he moved to Bristol, becoming an excise officer and later a teacher at the Fishponds free school.

The City of Bristol, at that time, was a centre for slave-trading and Hannah would, over time, become one of its staunchest critics.

The More's were a close family and all the sisters were educated at first by their father who taught them Latin and mathematics. Hannah was also taught French by her elder sisters. Her conversational French was improved by time spent with French prisoners of war from the Seven-Year's-War in Frenchay, then a small village near Bristol.

She was keen to learn, possessed a sharp intellect and was assiduous in studying and, according to family tradition, began writing at an early age.

In 1758 Jacob established his own girls' boarding school at Trinity Street in Bristol for the elder sisters, Mary and Elizabeth, to run. Hannah became a pupil there when she was 12. Jacob and his wife moved to Stony Hill in the city to open a school for boys.

Hannah became a teacher at her sister's school and it was here that she produced her first literary efforts. These were prompted by trying to find material suitable for her young charges to act in. Her first, written in 1762, was The Search after Happiness (by the mid-1780s some 10,000 copies had been sold).

In 1767 Hannah gave up her share in the school to become engaged to William Turner. After six years, with no wedding in sight, and Turner reluctant to move forward, the engagement was broken off. It was now 1773 and by all accounts Hannah suffered a nervous breakdown and spent some time recuperating in nearby Uphill. Turner then bestowed upon her an annual annuity of £200. This was enough to meet her needs and set her free to pursue a literary career. With that ambition London was her next stop. She travelled there in the winter of 1773/74 together with her sisters, Sarah and Martha.

She had previously written some verses on a production of King Lear staged by the famous actor David Garrick and this led to a lasting friendship with him and a pivotal introduction to the London Literary society. Now she met and charmed Samuel Johnson, Joshua Reynolds and Edmund Burke. Johnson is quoted as saying to her "Madam, before you flatter a man so grossly to his face, you should consider whether or not your flattery is worth having." He would later be quoted as calling her "the finest versifatrix in the English language".

Hannah also became a leading member of the Bluestocking group of women who met to further literary and intellectual pursuits. Here she met women who were to become life-long friends; Elizabeth Montagu, Frances Boscawen, Elizabeth Carter, Elizabeth Vesey and Hester Chapone (Hannah later wrote a celebration of this circle in her 1782 poem The Bas Bleu, or, Conversation, published in 1784).

Her first play, The Inflexible Captive, was staged at Bath in 1775. It was based on the opera, Attilio Regulo, by the Italian Pietro Metastasio (1698-1782) whose works she admired.

Her theatrical career was now in full swing. David Garrick himself produced her next play, Percy, in 1777 as well as writing both the Prologue and Epilogue for it. It was a great success when performed at Covent Garden in December of that year. Her next play, Fatal Falsehood, was staged in 1779, shortly after the death of Garrick. It was less successful but still admired.

With David Garrick now passed (January 20th, 1779) Hannah came to view the theatre as both morally wrong and not where her ambitions now lay. She now began to spend her time advancing her interests in other areas.

In 1781 she first met Horace Walpole, man of letters art historian and Whig politician and now corresponded regularly with him.

A friendship with James Oglethorpe, who had long been concerned with slavery as a moral issue and who was working with Granville Sharp in an early abolitionist capacity, started to awaken Hannah's social conscious.

Hannah turned to religious writing, beginning with her Sacred Dramas in 1782; it rapidly ran through nineteen editions. These and the poems Bas-Bleu and Florio (1786) mark her gradual transition to a more serious and considered view of life and are fully expressed in her Thoughts on the Importance of the Manners of the Great to General Society (1788), and An Estimate of the Religion of the Fashionable World (1790).

In Bristol, in 1784, she discovered the poet Ann Yearsley, the so-called 'poetical milkmaid of Bristol'. With Yearsley destitute, Hannah raised a considerable sum of money for her. Lactilia, as Yearsley was known, published Poems, on Several Occasions in 1785, earning about £600. Hannah and Elizabeth Montagu held the profits in trust to protect them from Yearsley's husband. However Ann wished for the capital to be made over, and made insinuations of stealing against Hannah. The money was released and Hannah felt her reputation had been tarnished.

With the death of Samuel Johnson in December 1784, Hannah moved, with her sister Martha, in 1795, to a cottage at Cowslip Green, near Wrington in rural Somerset, "to escape from the world gradually".

In the summer of 1786, she spent time with Sir Charles and Lady Margaret Middleton at their home in Teston in Kent. Among their guests was the local vicar James Ramsay and a young Thomas Clarkson, both of whom were central to the early abolition campaign against slavery.

In 1787, she met John Newton and the 'Clapham Sect' (a group of wealthy evangelical Christians who lived near Clapham and met at Henry Thornton's house). The group was strongly opposed to the Slave Trade. William Wilberforce was a member of the group and he and Hannah became firm friends.

Hannah contributed much to the running of the newly-founded Abolition Society including, in February 1788, her publication of Slavery, a Poem which has long been recognised as one of the most important poems of the abolition period. The poem dramatically described a mistreated, enslaved female separated from her children and severely questioned Britain's role in the Slave Trade.

Her relationship with members of the society, especially Wilberforce, was close. She spent the summer of 1789 holidaying with Wilberforce in the Peak District, planning for the abolition campaign, which, at the time, was at its height.

Her work now became more evangelical. In the 1790s she wrote several Cheap Repository Tracts which covered moral, religious and political topics and were both for sale or distributed to literate poor people. This coincided with her increasing philanthropic work in the Mendip area.

Beyond any doubt, Hannah was the most influential female member of the Society for Effecting the Abolition of the African Slave Trade.

Hannah wrote many ethical books and tracts: Strictures on the Modern System of Female Education (1799), Hints towards Forming the Character of a Young Princess (1805), Cœlebs in Search of a Wife (only nominally a story, 1809), Practical Piety (1811), Christian Morals (1813), Character of St Paul (1815), Moral Sketches (1819). She was a rapid writer, and her work is consequently discursive, animated and without a rigorous structure.

However the originality and force of Hannah's writings perhaps explains her extraordinary popularity. At the behest of Beilby Porteus, Bishop of London and a leading abolitionist, Hannah wrote many spirited rhymes and prose tales, the earliest of which was Village Politics, by Will Chip (1792), intended to counteract the doctrines of Thomas Paine and the influence of the French Revolution.

The series of Cheap Repository Tracts, eventually led to the formation of the Religious Tracts Society. The Tracts were produced at the rate of three a month between 1795 and 1797.

The most famous is perhaps The Shepherd of Salisbury Plain, describing a family of incredible frugality and contentment. Two million copies of these rapid and telling sketches were circulated, in one year, teaching the poor in rhetoric of the most ingenious homeliness to rely upon the virtues of content, sobriety, humility, industry and reverence for the British Constitution, hatred of the French, trust in God and in the kindness of the gentry.

Several of the Tracts oppose slavery and the slave trade, in particular, the poem The Sorrows of Yamba; or, The Negro Woman's Lamentation, which appeared in November 1795 and which was co-authored with Eaglesfield Smith. However, the tracts have also been noted for their encouragement of social quietism in an age of revolution.

In 1789, she purchased a small house at Cowslip Green in Somerset. Wilberforce encouraged Hannah to set up a Sunday school in Cheddar, where poor children could be taught to read. Soon she and her sisters had set up similar schools throughout the Mendip villages, despite fierce opposition.

She was instrumental in setting up twelve schools by 1800 where reading, the Bible and the catechism were taught to local children. Hannah also donated money to Bishop Philander Chase for the founding of Kenyon College, and a portrait of her hangs there in Peirce Hall.

John Scandrett Harford of Blaise Castle was a prodigious benefactor to More's schools in the 1790s, and Hannah modeled the idealised hero and heroine in Cœlebs in Search of Wife (1809) on Mr and Mrs Harford.

However it cannot be said that Hannah was a staunch supporter of Women's rights. She refused to read Mary Wollstonecraft's Rights of Women, saying "so many women are fond of government... because they are not fit for it. To be unstable and capricious is but too characteristic of our sex". She was also shocked by the movement for female education in France, saying "they run to study philosophy, and neglect their families to be present at lectures in anatomy". She is also said to have turned down an honorary membership of the Royal Society of Literature because she considered her "sex alone a disqualification".

The More sisters also met with a good deal of opposition in their philanthropic works: the farmers thought that education, even to the limited extent of learning to read, would be fatal to agriculture, and the clergy, whose neglect she was making good, accused her of Methodist tendencies.

She continued to oppose slavery throughout her life, but at the time of the Abolition Bill of 1807 (which outlawed the slave trade, but not slavery itself), her health did not permit her to take as active a role in the movement as she had done in the late 1780s, although she maintained a correspondence with Wilberforce and others Abolitionists.

In her later life, she continued to dedicate much of her time to religious writing. Nevertheless, her most popular work was a novel, Cœlebs in Search of a Wife, which appeared in two volumes in 1809 (and which ran to nine editions in 1809 alone).

In 1816, Hannah was still at odds with the French. Following Waterloo she is quoted as saying that 'peace with France is a worse evil than war', and refused to allow a French translation of Cœlebs.

Her last few years were spent at Clifton, people from all parts came to visit her even though her health was fading and she was writing less often.

She lived just long enough to see the act finally abolishing slavery. In July 1833, the Bill to abolish slavery throughout the British Empire passed in the House of Commons, followed by the House of Lords on August 1st.

Hannah More died on September 7th, 1833. She is buried at Church of All Saints, Wrington. In her will she left more than £30,000 to charities and religious societies, the equivalent today of many millions.